I0014586

FACEBOOK

Advanced 2.0

The Social Networking & Web Marketing Guide
for Internet & Computer Guru's Everywhere!

By

Ryan Wade Brown
www.RyanWadeBrown.com

INDEX

Preface

In this book we will be mostly discussing the rise of Facebook. The rise of Facebook has not only changed the course of the Internet, but it has also changed the course of marketing online. With a huge population of users, nearly 25 million users, and more and more being added on a daily basis, Facebook requires a tremendous amount of manpower to keep it running efficiently. It is interesting to get to the base of the website to actually understand what occurred over the period of time.

Like many other great businessmen, Mark Zuckerberg, has a tendency of being defiant in his life. He proved he was with his various ideas and thoughts over the course of his life time. It is an interesting fact to note that he was attending Harvard and had no idea or intention of creating a business from his dorm room. With the help of great minds in one location, Mark Zuckerberg created one of the world's most acknowledge and well-received websites throughout the internet. This website is not just an ordinary social networking website either.

The reasons behind why it became special and started rising in population are explained later on. The statistics speak for themselves in the chapters which are later on discussed.

The information which is provided in the later on chapters is both astonishing as well as completely unpredictable. Many marketing companies as well as other public relations company would not have dreamt of coming up with an idea which Mark Zuckerberg created.

We will also be going more into detail as to the recent controversies behind the various claims made behind Facebook. The entire idea of Facebook is unique and sets itself apart from the ordinary Social networking MySpace. Even though it may have been released at a later period, Facebook has left these social networking websites back in the dust. Now the real question is, where will this unique idea take the rest of us in the near future?

What is Facebook?

Emergence of the internet brought the entire world on a single platform. Nowadays, people from every part of the globe are sharing their successes, failures, discoveries, inventions, and many others with everyone. The purpose of the whole idea is to unite the entire world. However, when the internet was initially started, nobody had anything like Facebook in mind. It was seen as a mode to simplify the business related issues. The internet evolution brought many other things to human life, rather than just business solutions.

During the evolution of internet, the concept of "social networking" emerged. The concept was not new as it has been used in a different context; however, the internet was not used for the socializing purposes. As the internet started invading human lives, they started feeling the need of staying in touch all the time and from anywhere in the world. This laid the basis for the social networking websites. Initially, websites were developed which had the basic connectivity to the loved ones or the people they knew. These website were extremely restricted. Although, at that time these websites were the best known technology and served their purpose effectively.

FACEBOOK ADVANCED 2.0

As the discoveries in the field of internet continued to happen, the social networking websites became more user friendly and effective to build relationships.

In 2004, Facebook emerged as one of social networking website. Nowadays, people from all over the world use Facebook to stay in touch with their friends, family, and peers. It is not restricted to businesses or people for a specific age. Students, employees, housewives, and people from every profession are using Facebook to maintain good relationships. Due to its huge user base and intellectual activities, it is known as the "thinking person's" social network. Facebook is not the only social network website on the internet; there are many others as well. However, Facebook managed to get the second largest social website of the world in no time. Before Facebook, social networking websites were only providing a platform. It is up to the user, how they use it. However, Facebook came in with a different vision that is to provide the best platform to the world, with a direction to every single user. Every user can get any kind of information or relationship they want. They can socialize with people with similar interests and from all over the world.

History

Facebook was started by a Harvard sophomore, Mark Zuckerberg, in May 2004. It was initially started by a few friends to stay in touch with each other and to create a better understanding among college students. The name, Facebook, came from the publication that most of the colleges distributes to the students, a Yearbook. It was created so that they can develop a better understanding among each other and now these publications are more commonly known as Facebook.

Therefore, Mark Zuckerberg thought to serve the purpose of these publications over the internet. It was first launched as a networking system within the campus. Therefore, his friends were among the early users of "The Facebook". He used to run this project as his hobby like other Harvard students. He never thought that his project will become one of the most successful projects in the history of internet. Within a few months, Facebook became the hottest issue in the campus. Due to its success and rapid growth, it was launched to other colleges, high schools, and then to the general public. However, it was restricted to the users who were 13 or older.

FACEBOOK ADVANCED 2.0

It looks easy and simple; however, Mark Zuckerberg faced a lot of troubles and difficulties for making it what we have presently. Before launching Facebook, Mark Zuckerberg was an early and active member of houseSYSTEM, which was established by Greenspan. HouseSYSTEM was the service provided to the Harvard student foe college related activities. Mark Zuckerberg received an email from Greenspan about his project. After knowing "the Facebook" project, Greenspan wanted Mark Zuckerberg to integrate the both systems. However, Mark Zuckerberg decided to run the system alone. His ambition to make it a huge success took him to, Silicon Valley. There he was able to raise enough capital to fund his project. It was Mark Zuckerberg who had the vision to transfer this networking websites for college students in the United States, into a worldwide service for both personal and business use.

Furthermore, Mark Zuckerberg did not carry out the project alone. After realizing the success of "the Facebook", two of his Harvard fellows Dustin Moskovitz and Chris Hughes joined him. The students dropped out of Harvard to run the Facebook as a fulltime business activity.

One more thing that which made the success of Facebook possible was its registration criteria.

Initially, it was not available to everyone in United States.

To use Facebook, the person had to be enrolled in one of the 30,000 recognized schools, colleges, universities, or organizations within the United States and Canada. People from other English speaking countries were also allowed to join Facebook. This enabled Facebook to make good use of referral programs which laid the base of a strong Facebook network. In 2005, it was officially named as "Facebook" and the domain facebook.com was bought.

Facebook then started customizing its features and WebPages according to the needs and interests of each user. For that purpose studies regarding users preferences were carried out. This also helped Facebook to segregate the users on the basis of their demographic, geographic, and psychographic factors. Initially, marketers were in a habit to market their products over the internet without a careful analysis of their target market. That proved not to be a successful method to achieve desired results. Facebook was already the focus of marketers for its huge user base; however, when Facebook started to provide most accurate target customers to the marketers, it seemed as their dreams had come true.

With that Facebook obtained the perfect business model to pursue with.

For that reason, it expanded its network to the rest of the countries and customizing the service according to the need and language of that country. Facebook has been trying to provide the most desired services and technologies, as it is involving other related businesses into its service. Facebook gets convenient for the user to get everything at one single place.

Facebook has been providing the additional or extended version of its services on a step by step approach, this keeps the users retained. Also, they feel that they are getting the desired value for the time they have spent with Facebook. Facebook is expected to obtain the status of the largest social networking website by the end of this year.

Creator

A Harvard student, Mark Zuckerberg, created Facebook as part of his hobby when he was a sophomore. He never had the idea that his project will make a significant part in the history of the internet. Mark Zuckerberg is a computer programmer; he created Facebook with the help of his college students and roommates in Harvard. He is rated as one of the most successful entrepreneurs in America.

For his contribution to the internet and social networking, Time magazine has listed him amongst the most influential people of 2008.

Mark Zuckerberg was born in New York and he was brought up in Florida with his parents. Zuckerberg was inclined towards computer programming from the beginning. He started making communication tools and computer games at an early age, despite the fact that both of his parents were doctors. When he was in high school, he stared programming. His fist success came to his life, when Microsoft and AOL recruited Zuckerberg after purchasing his invention, which was a music player. However, he attended Harvard instead of joining these business giants.

Zuckerberg kept on experimenting with his programming skills and while staying at Harvard he created "coursematch"; the website was a design to give information about other students that were enrolled in the college. To protest against the absence of an image dictionary for college students, Zuckerberg created Facemash.com, which was an image rating site for Harvard students. However, his project remained available just for four hours, after he was caught by university administration. He was charged for violating the computer security and intellectual property rights of the university.

Moving along, he created a web portal to facilitate all the students preparing for final exams.

The web portal provided the notes to the students, which become the main mode of studying as the student's performance excelled using that web portal.

Zuckerberg left Harvard when he had to move to California to launch the Facebook. Some of his friends who helped him in the development and execution of the project moved along with him. They had the plan to move back to the college at the end of that year. However, after establishing the business they have not enrolled back into Harvard yet.

They first rented a small house to set it as their office. During the same season that they moved to California, Zuckerberg met Peter Thiel. Peter Thiel is the co-founder of Pay-Pal. They convinced him to invest in their company, as they had not enough capital at that time. Its acceptability among all the various age groups stimulated the growth of the company; nowadays, it has seventeen office buildings.

Users

Facebook was initially started as a web portal for students. It was intended to profile the graduates recently enrolled along with Zuckerberg.

Furthermore, the convenience and friendliness of the website brought many other people to log in. However, the project did not have the idea of going global in future, it was just to facilitate the new students to better understand and communicate with each other more effectively.

Since then, it has replaced the traditional college system of distributing papers to freshmen, focusing on the students and faculty. Its user base grew rapidly as older student found it easier and convenient to stay in contact with their other friends and relatives. Besides, it provided support to the faculty to inform communicate to the students as well. Therefore within 24 hours of its launch, 1,200 users' logged in. With this jumpstart, Facebook started its operation with the intention of using it as a university project. However in 2006, it was made to cover the users beyond the education industry.

Referral programs were basically used to stimulate the user's traffic of the Facebook. Every person who has an account with Facebook can refer his friends and other relatives. Initially it was restricted to the United State's schools and colleges only. However, when Facebook started its operations to the rest of the world, the referral program was extended across the boundaries of the United States.

Users from Harvard business school were amongst the first ones to use Facebook; however, it was then further provided to more than 300,000 colleges, high schools, and universities in the United States and Canada.

Acceptability of Facebook pushed the team to provide the social networking services to other English speaking countries as well.

As the company grew bigger, it expanded to other regions as well. When they realized the fact that customization is the most preferred factor of the users. They started customizing the services according to the language and the culture of that region. Therefore, Facebook has more than 35 translations available on the website, which can be used according to the need of that specific area. With the geographic expansion of Facebook, it has 60 translations in the development process. Besides the fact that it started from the United States, it has only 30% of its users from the United States. The rest of the 70% of users belong to the rest of the world.

Nowadays, more than 150 million users are registered on Facebook, which shows the tremendous growth of the website over the last few years. Besides that, half of the users of the Facebook are not even from colleges. This proves its acceptability and use to other professions as well.

The astonishing fact is that people more than 25 years of age and older make the greatest proportion of the Facebook users.

Managing such a huge number of users is not that easy, on Facebook 100 friends are listed in the friend list of an average user. All these users are managed by making their networks and categorizing them by their interests and age groups. Besides every user is given the option of customizing their page and applications; which help them to stay clean and organized.

Platform

Facebook has to provide the best services to its users in order to keep growing and to retain them for a longer period of time. However, for that a lot of programming and development is required. The creator of Facebook announced a platform for its activities, where programmers can make and send applications to Facebook. Programmers from different parts of the world are actively participating to maintain the platform of Facebook.

Besides this, their relationships within the local area help them to better understand the local culture and to translate it in the form of applications.

Otherwise it might not look good if the application goes against the culture or does not fit in with the local culture of that area. Also, programmers from all over the world bring new ideas to Facebook on daily basis. Not all of them get selected since the marketing analysts prioritize the applications that need to be developed and launched.

The platform does not only provide the facility to the programmers to work for Facebook. Therefore, entrepreneurs from all over the world are also invited to work for Facebook. However, these entrepreneurs should belong to the related industry and should add value to the Facebook. More than 660,000 entrepreneurs and programmers representing 180 countries are working on the platform of Facebook. Due to Facebook, programmers are able to provide more than 52,000 applications to its users and 140 new applications are added per day on an average.

However, due to the quality and the logic of the applications, only 95% of the applications are being used by Facebook users.

It is not all about the programming but also the logic behind these applications increase their effectiveness and acceptability. With that, Facebook is seen as the most promising social networking website. Other websites lost their users due to their monotonous nature and look. The platform of Facebook enables it to provide new features and applications every day.

Features

Facebook was developed with an aim to provide connectivity along with entertainment. Connectivity is not the big deal, there are many other websites offering the same service. It is the way you provide it; users do not feel bored while using Facebook. Most of the time users get caught up within the many different features of Facebook. Sometimes they even end up forgetting their reasons as to why they logged in. However, other websites just offer the basic feature of connectivity; not even showing much importance to the special events of a user's life.

Features on Facebook are designed according to the needs of the users. The main features of Facebook includes the wall, poke, new feeds, status update, photos and instant messaging. All these features connect the users with their friends and others.

Headquarters

Facebook has its headquarters in two specific regions to provide the best possible services to its users. The ole of these headquarters is to synchronize the activities and operations of subsidiaries of Facebook. However, these headquarters are aimed to provide up to date information and analysis for the future course of actions. Major decisions and concerns are handled by these four headquarters. The most essential part while deciding about the strength of the company and future course of action is to also provide businesses intelligence from these headquarters. Business intelligence includes Executives, Reports, Industry, Products, History, Financials, Competitors, and Subsidiary locations. The two major regions where Facebook has its headquarters are:

Palo Alto, California

California is the most populous city of United States. It is famous for its contribution in the field of science and technology. It is ranked among the 10 largest economies of world.

Palo Alto is the charter city of California and is located in the San Francisco Bay area of the state. Silicon Valley is known for its business activities and is home to several other high technology companies. Besides Facebook's residence there, Hewlett-Packard is one of the companies headquarter in Palo Alto. The city is also famous as it includes the portions of the world renowned Stanford University.

Headquarters of Facebook located in California, United States are responsible for monitoring and controlling all the activities of Facebook subsidiaries located within the American region. However, regions other than America are also monitored by the same headquarter.

Dublin, Ireland

Dublin is the capital of Ireland and is also the capital of the country. Dublin is considered to be the most important place in the history of Ireland. Besides, it is the economic, cultural and technological center of Ireland.

Dublin has the greatest population growth rate among other European cities.

Facebook is also headquartered in Dublin and is responsible to ensure the efficiency and effectiveness of subsidiaries located in the European region. With careful monitoring and organization from their headquarters in Dublin, Facebook is able to provide its superior services in the European region as well.

Funding

Facebook was initially started with the funding from co-founder of Pay-Pal, Peter Thiel. He invested US $500,000 in Facebook as an initial investment. However, later on Facebook received another $12.7 million in venture capital from Accel Partners. Accel Partners is a private equity company, which invests into the software and networking sectors. The firm is headquartered in the same city of Palo Alto, where Facebook has headquarters for the American region. As the Facebook grew further, it received another investment of $27.5 million from Greylock Partners, which is also a venture capital firm. Facebook continued receiving funding with its expansion. Microsoft has reported to invest in Facebook against 1.6% share of Facebook. Microsoft has paid $246 million to get that much amount of share in Facebook.

Besides, in 2007, a Hong Kong billionaire Li-Ka Shing invested another $60 million in Facebook.

Facebook does not rely on the investment from private sector only; however, they have developed a very successful business model to ensure the proper funding for Facebook. With such a large customer base, Facebook is able to approach as many people as it possibly can throughout the world. However, Facebook does not have to spend extra money for that; it is the part of its operations. The capacity of Facebook to reach such a strong and huge user base sparked the marketers to communicate their message through Facebook. Therefore, Facebook offered them to place their advertisements on the website, which will be provided to their exact target market. Since Facebook has a clear and accurate record of the people using Facebook, this business model of Facebook has been proved to be the most successful for internet marketing and therefore, it is generating huge funds for Facebook.

Comparison to Other Social Networking Websites

When you think of the first few social networks one of the names that probably pops up in your mind is MySpace. However, when you think of the top ranking social networks, Facebook is number one. Facebook has gained so much popularity ever since it opened up for users that weren't college students. Over the months, it has experienced a flood of new users. This was boosted even further by the launch of Facebook applications. Now which one of these two is on top of its game?

The Design

First, we will examine the designs of both networks. Now Facebook has a better layout than MySpace. That is because Facebook profiles are set up well and are easier to navigate through. This makes it much more efficient for users and it becomes easier to get the information that you want. The MySpace profiles are not as neat and they are very inconsistent with efficiency.

When comparing the overall site design, MySpace looks unprofessional when compared to Facebook. This is due to the inconsistent design of MySpace. The MySpace admin makes the site difficult to use for their users.

Now, when we look at the profiles between Facebook and MySpace, they are about the same. However, when people were surveyed on which default profile looks better, Facebook won again because it looks neater. They even tie in customization. Facebook lets you add and remove applications. MySpace lets you do whatever you want with the pages. However, with MySpace you have to have some knowledge of HTML. This is the reason why MySpace's design is unruly, since not many people are experienced with HTML.

Both sites are very well organized but still, Facebook is the winner because it has clean layouts that allow users to find everything easily. Its start page is a link to all the info you need in neat and tidy boxes. So the Winner of this round is ….. **Facebook!**

Effect on the Media

Facebook has well-organized pictures in a section that also allows the users to tag people and have other people tag them. With this new application, which was recently released, you can now add Flicker and other photo sharing site streams to your profile. Now Fox Company owns Photobucket, which provides photo hosting to MySpace users only.

There really is no reason to compare the two on video quality. MySpace and Facebook both let you upload videos and they both run on their own flash player. MySpace will allow you to embed videos on your profile. However, you can not post any single video to a Facebook profile page for visitors; this works in favor of Facebook as it avoids unexpected videos.

In music, MySpace wins. This is because every band has a MySpace account. On Facebook, you can only add your data from music tracking sites like iLike and Last.FM. This is also done through apps. Currently, this is the most popular application on Facebook.

Facebook has a slight advantage in network sharing. It allows you to share media links with easy through the Facebook feed. This is one thing that many MySpace users would love to be able to do. In MySpace, you can only grab embedded media links, like videos from other profiles to repost on your MySpace profile. This round again, goes to Facebook.

Community

Now there is a huge difference here between the two networks in this category. Facebook users add only their real friends. MySpace makes it seem like a contest where everyone is trying to have the biggest friends' list.

In Facebook, it is not about the quantity of friends but rather quality of friends. Users that want to get in touch with people they really know utilize Facebook. Then they share posts with them.

Both sites make special groups. Only Facebook makes the groups more prominent. They are a huge part of the service that is being provided. A lot of people are using these groups for clever reasons, like planning an event or giving the inside scope to fans.

It's hard to keep track of new stuff on MySpace. This is where Facebook smashes MySpace. MySpace makes it hard to know what your friends did to their profiles and what they have added. To find out you must go and look at their profile on a daily basis. The only way to find out if someone has added you on MySpace is to look for your picture on his or her list. And if you add a friend, you must look for them on your list. Now Facebook has two feeds, one tells you what's new with you. For example, who accepted your friend request, items you posted, etc. The other feed informs you about all your friends, who they added and what groups they joined.

Both are adequate in messaging. Both networks have a place where people can leave messages on their friends' profile and they both have a basic e-mail system.

Facebook has a system where you can connect with co-workers. This enables you to see what's new with them. Now you could even create a network for your company. MySpace was only designed for teens, so it does not really have these types of features.

Which Network is More Useful?

One of the biggest reasons why people join social networks is to reconnect with their old friends or classmates. Facebook makes this a lot easier because the whole site is organized by schools and by locations too. All you need is to remember your friends name and you will probably find them if they have an account. MySpace lets you search or school friends but it doesn't put any emphasis on real friendship.

Facebook is now one of the best ways to contact people if you are unable to find any information on them. People are now more likely to notice a message on Facebook than MySpace messages because there is less Facebook spam.

If you want to promote yourself, I would suggest MySpace. Hundreds of bands use MySpace to promote their music and their fans use it to show them support. This doesn't happen as much on Facebook. However, groups allow companies to promote themselves.

Now here is the interesting part. If you want to go on a date with someone who is hot, you should use MySpace. Using MySpace will help you sleep with people more often. I don't believe that this happens with Facebook, it's just not that probable. So I guess this round goes to MySpace.

Which is Easier to Use?

When it comes to adding friends, MySpace usually wins. This is because adding friends and accepting friend requests only takes one single click. The major advantage over Facebook is that you can add many friends at once on MySpace. For some odd reason, this was never added on Facebook.

When it comes to search engines, it makes me laugh. Google ends up doing the search for the loser here. Facebook's search engine beats MySpace by a landslide. Google is providing the info for MySpace search; its results are useless compared to Facebook's. MySpace's search looks in the whole entire profile, even if it's looking for just one person. Facebook's search is smart enough to know if you are looking for a user, movie, or someone's interests.

MySpace and Facebook both have pretty decent navigation system, but MySpace can't match up to Facebook because face book is specific and much more accurate in pulling out profiles.

Now Facebook makes it easy to hide information from certain people and to not show any information that is considered private. If you only want your friends to see your contact information, then it only takes a second to set that up. MySpace has privacy too but it doesn't compare to Facebook's. We all can see that face book wins this round.

Now if you tally up the score you can see that Facebook is much better than MySpace and other outdated social networks. MySpace was great while it lasted but the developers got lazy and stopped expanding it. Facebook is getting popular and it just barely started to accept people who aren't in college. So if you don't have a Facebook profile goes make one right now.

FACEBOOK ADVANCED 2.0

The Many Different Uses of Facebook

Facebook was created by Mark Zuckerburg with the intention to give people the ability to share and to make the world feel as though it more connected and open with one another. There are nearly millions of people from all over the world that are using Facebook everyday in order to keep in touch with so many friends. There are many different applications and uses for this website. Over the last few years, this website has gained a lot of popularity amongst people of all ages. It is also been named the second most visited website daily.

Since there are so many people on Facebook that are using it and updating it daily, it is a great professional networking tool as well as a great social networking tool. Facebook was designed originally as way of gathering friends and keeping in touch with them by a student from Harvard.

There are many different uses for Facebook which people have come up with over the past few years. The most basic type of use of Facebook is to keep in touch with daily friends and contacts by always staying in direct touch.

FACEBOOK ADVANCED 2.0

Facebook makes it easy for a person to communicate to someone else, it only takes a few minutes and it has replaced the way we talk on the phone. Other ways of using Facebook include the photo albums which you can place on there, as well as the fact that you can share interesting links or websites with other people. There is also the option of uploading videos and sharing videos from other websites with your friends and family members. You can easily learn more about the previous people you may have met once in a while as well as the people you hope to meet later on. Facebook was started as a social networking tool for the kids in Harvard, but now it is being used as a professional networking tool. There are also many other uses that have developed over the past few years, making Facebook even more important better than what is out there.

Point is that everyone can find a use for Facebook in their lives. It doesn't matter what that person man do, but Facebook is something where everyone feels like they are at home. The truth is that your profile page is a way of expressing everything about you. You can voice whatever you want about whomever, whenever you want. There are some restrictions, which fall under harassing others or harming others, but overall it is a pleasant site for any mature human being.

Advertising

The option of Facebook is absolutely free and ready to be used by anyone and everyone. This means that it has become a great opportunity for marketers to really get close to the "consumers" or the people who use their brands. The type of research that Facebook provides businesses is extremely beneficial to the company. Not only are the able to see how many members or groups are created for a certain movie or television show, but they are also able to see their views and opinions. With the help of technology and the ability to share links and videos online, especially the easiness of it on Facebook, many people are able to voice their opinions and then either share it or place it directly on Facebook for others to see. These marketing opportunities are irresistible to almost every type of business man.

There are no biased reviews since there is no actual formal interview or research being conducted. The researchers are more of observers that can easily view the opinions of their fans and also the criticism of all else. The people do not have to worry about pleasing anyone; they can just voice their opinion out in the public without having to worry about the consequences. There is no need to please the interviewer, to answer long questionnaires or even fill out a survey of any sort.

Thanks to the technology nowadays, there is no need to ask anything as a business man. This also saves you the time and money from having to collect all information as well. The cost of conducting research does take a lot of time and money, but with the ease of Facebook, you can gather information quite efficiently.

Most actors or actresses, even comedians, have some type of "fan page". On that fan page, anyone can come up and talk about anything they want. They can criticize them for the work they may have done and be completely honest and blunt about it. They can also appraise them for what they have done in the past. They are able to see how the real world views them through the different discussions, spoofs, and other creative types of information placed throughout Facebook. Sometimes the fact that it may *not* be discussed amongst Facebook users may be a sign of its own.

Nearly more than 25 million users have joined Facebook since its launch. This means that there are nearly 25 million consumers and fans are just voicing their opinion over the internet, especially on Facebook. They voice their opinions by creating different groups, people can usually find at least one, but often times there are dozens set up around any random topic.

The different groups are created due to the different opinions that people may have, some may have love for a specific person, while others may hate them. The ease of joining these groups and posting anything within that specific group, or even writing a whole blog in regards to that topic, all takes nearly just one click and is extremely easy for anyone.

Recently Facebook came up with a new way of generating quick surveys. Facebook Polls is a quick and easy way to ask questions to any and all of Facebook users. This program can easily target either all of the Facebook users, or may even segment the population of Facebooking depending on various characteristics, factors, or options. Some of the more common ways differentiating target customers is by their age, geography, gender, or what groups they might belong to. The cost and the ease, of using such a program, is nearly around five dollars, which is still a very low cost compared to other advertising opportunities. There is also a cost per response, which is a very low cost and can easily be taken care of companies. This is one of the really quick and easy ways of researching a large scale of consumers for advertising companies in a short while in order to see what their fans may really think about their products.

One important factor which remains a mystery is the way that Facebook is heading forward into technology. Now that almost any user can create their own applications and then upload them for people to use, Facebook is going to be different. Some people predict Facebook to be on its way to becoming the next big web giant. Facebook will not be just any ordinary networking website or regular website, but rather a system or platform which has the ability to create sub-networks for social networking purposes. Sub-networks which help people come together for the common goal as one, no matter how far apart they may be.

Politics

Another great way of using Facebook is to use it as a political campaigning tool in order to attract the next generation of voters. Politics pay a major role in Facebook as many people are able to voice their political choice just on their profile page. By appealing to the younger generation of voters with Facebook, nominees are able to really get a more personalized response. Just recently with the November elections that occurred and went through with a takeover of the Democratic party over Congress, a lot of it was a result from the increase of political activity occurring on Facebook. The result came from the rapid increase in voting from the younger citizens.

The citizens between the ages of 18 to 24 are considered to have the lowest voting records compared to any other age bracket. Even then, many politicians were able to use Facebook to their advantage and started creating a profile in order to appeal to the younger generation for their votes.

Since students spend almost all of their free time that they have, and some even take the time out to use the internet and browse through Facebook, politicians really grasped the idea of attracting the younger generation. By being able to create an online profile, they were able to create and raise awareness of the potential supporters from their campaigning platforms and plans for office. This was a great way in order to spread the word to all types of college students and citizens above 18, by showing that they can understand and take interest in the same things as them. It shows that the candidate is slightly liberal and is able to focus on more down to earth topics, which is like creating a bond directly with the average college students. This is a great way to utilize Facebook compared to other social networking, since there are so many mature and serious users signed up.

Promoting

Another great way of using Facebook and a common way which can be seen on Facebook, is the fact that people can easily promote their own band or career. These solo artists or bands are able to create groups and events in order to start gathering a fan base from all parts of the world and start letting people know about the upcoming performances that they might be holding. It gives the people a general idea of what type of music your band plays, as well as how you are overall. There are easy ways of setting up demo's, uploading videos, as well as uploading and publishing photographs of one's own band performing. As a new performer penetrating an already competitive market, it is extremely important to be distinct and unique, and the best way of doing that is to promote your own style of music and define the uniqueness over Facebook. People are able to get all the publicity that they require from Facebook and use it for their own benefit. The best part of it all is that it is all free, which saves money to spend on recording in a studio. Once a person is discovered, they'll surely thank Facebook fans.

Education

Education is a major part of Facebook. Information is spread rapidly as well as breaking news. Groups are created randomly and are usually kept up to date in regards with the breaking news, which includes current events as they occur throughout the world. There are many groups that have been created due to the war and killings throughout the world in order to try and prevent it and voice out to the politicians of this world, as well as creating a bond within their friend groups.

Another great way of using Facebook is for professors and teachers to able to communicate with their students. By being able to create a group or an online grade book, they can continue their classroom on to a virtual classroom where they can post supplement reading and notes. Sometimes students are unable to come to class due to sicknesses or other reasons, and thus them and up missing lectures and assignments. By using Facebook to keep everyone on the same page at all times is a great idea. The class can all get together and participate openly in ongoing discussions as well as voice their opinions without having to take a lot of time out.

Sometimes teachers have to cut lectures short, or maybe are unable to come to class on a specific date. By just updating the information and sending out a message to all Facebook group members, the information is spread out easily and thus makes it all convenient for everyone. Teachers can continue to have a relationship or a bond with the students, where the students can express their problems and troubles with the class work or have any questions regarding previous lectures. Since most of the students are already on Facebook, having it become a part of the class participation, students will appreciate the time and effort that the teacher may take out for them. This makes the student feel better and more excited about learning new things in a new manner, a manner which has never been done before.

Overall, there are many different uses for Facebook. Facebook offers a very clean and mature environment in which can you be personal, but still be professional. The style of Facebook profile pages prevents users from doing or adding things which may seem inappropriate to others. Facebook is not exactly like all other social networking sites, since it is not just for college students or even just students.

Facebook has so many different uses that anyone and everyone can somehow benefit from it like many politicians, musicians, teachers, professors, and students already do. By employing new and alternative uses within Facebook, there is an easier way to target a large number of people, including the core audience, and to take control as well as make others understand the importance of their opinion. Like all opinions, there will be criticism, but it can all be handled in a mature and gentle manner, in an adult like manner on a virtual space.

Rise of Facebook

Facebook has become the most popular and used website over the internet in just 2 to 5 years. However, if we compare Microsoft with Facebook, we get to know that even Microsoft has not experienced such a massive growth in the limited time like the Facebook did. There are several reasons that can be mentioned as the success factors of Facebook. However, the launch of Facebook was so perfect that it gave it a jump start to grow, which is endless. Facebook offers 'newness', every time you log in, you come to know that there is something new waiting for you, this was not the case with the previous social networking websites. People used those websites just to send messages to each other for the purpose of connectivity. This is what made Facebook unique since Facebook came up with the idea of innovative entertainment along with best connectivity options. Innovation is only one of the many aspects of Facebook that can be identified as the reason of its popularity.

Besides, Facebook provides its users with increased level of convenience. People using Facebook never complained about getting stuck with the website. However, the previous version of social networking websites has been really heavy and time consuming. Using the most recent technology available, Facebook has been able to provide its users the convenience that they have been dreaming of. Convenience does not really mean working on websites, traditional social networking websites required to fill lengthy user information forms. However, Facebook introduced referral programs, where you can make your friends user of Facebook by just one click. You can do anything you want to without any difficulty or interruption.

Facebook is tailored according to the need of individual users. This may become impossible, if the Facebook has to do that much personalization. However, to counter this, Facebook used the idea to personalizing the webpage by individual users as per their requirements and interest. This helps the users to make the service user friendly for themselves. Besides, the technology used by Facebook does not consume much time to use any of the available option. People using Facebook can connect to their friends who are using some other service like MSN. The objective of this feature is to give the possible friendliness services to the users.

The layout of Facebook is very simple, as the website with crowded layout affects the very purpose of the service. The first page of Facebook is the log-in page, where the user can easily register just by providing a name, password, and a valid email address. Facebook then automatically generates the list of your friends using other services like MSN, Yahoo, Gmail, and AOL. The list is then provided to the user to invite these friends to become the part of Facebook users as well. If most of these friends are already available on Facebook, then Facebook begins to inform you of such friends that you might consider adding. The homepage layout totally depends on the user with little space cover by Facebook. The cover space provides the menu at the header and toolbar at the footer. Besides those, the left and right sides are designed as strips dedicated for minor advertisements.

Compared with other websites, the web design of the Facebook is very simple yet attractive. Most of the websites tried to provide maximum applications; however, they ignore the convenience and appealing factors of the web design. Color scheme of Facebook is very attractive and does not offend any gender or culture of the world.

However, people can personalize their homepage as per their taste and needs. With that, the homepage of the website provides the updated information about your friends and any other activity that has something relevant for you. On the right side of the homepage, you will find space for requests, applications, birthday alerts and options to invite your friends. Therefore, the right side of the homepage acts as reminder for you, providing you information about upcoming events and applications. On the left side of the page tabs of new feeds, status updates, posted items, photos, and live feed are provided. However, the number and nature of tabs depends on the kind of applications you are using. This enhances the ability of the user to get updates right on the homepage before he moves to the other parts of the website.

There are several applications and features used by the people registered on Facebook. This would have made the Facebook very hard to browse or use. However, using a very efficient navigation system, Facebook users are able to navigate through the entire website conveniently and comfortably. Basic features of Facebook are provided on the main menu of the website including the homepage, friends, profile and inbox. Users cannot change these options, as these options are mandatory to run the account on Facebook.

Application toolbars provided in the footer provides the options of advertising, developers, jobs, terms, find friends, privacy, account, about, and help. These options are provided on the homepage in order to provide the desired comfort level to the users. However, navigating throuhh the website you will find that every page is designed with these baisc features provided by Facebook, however the theme of the page can eaisly be changed by users.

Facebook has been adding several different features and applications as the need for them became imperative. Facebook Chat was not part of the website before; however, when Facebook realized that people need to talk online instantly to their friends and family while using Facebook. Using other options for chat became difficult for them; therefore, Facebook added the chat options to its website. Facebook chat is provided with very simple features, as with extra features the chat will be affected. People would not get quality chat in presence of these features. However, people gave a very good response to the Facebook chat. Also like other social networking websites, users do not have to download the software for Facebook chat. Options for Facebook chat is provided on the homepage, where you can check your online friends and talk to them with a single click.

To further provide support and convenience to users, Facebook has provided an option of Facebook mobile. Using Facebook mobile, users can easily login to Facebook using their personal mobiles. To activate the option you have to provide the mobile information on Facebook, Facebook will then send you a code to verify that it is your personal mobile. Friend search, adding friends to the friend lists, pokes, messages, and status updates are the options provided by Facebook mobile. Otherwise, it will get difficult for users to browse the whole website using their mobiles.

All these features that have been updated every day on Facebook became the reason for the success of Facebook. However, using Facebook you will find that there several other reasons adding into the popularity of Facebook. Every page will have more than one reason to attract or captivate you. That is the reason why Facebook is so popular today. One can never list all the reasons contributing to the success of Facebook. As Facebook is not a general social network website, it is one of the most personalized social websites over the internet. Many applications may not captivate you, as they are not created specifically for you. Therefore, it is very hard to state one single application, feature, or service as the success factor of the Facebook.

However, most of the people state the personalization is a more innovative manner as the success factor of Facebook.

Considering other uses of Facebook besides making friends, you will realize that it can also be served as job portal. There are accounts and groups of several different multinationals, to whom you can communicate to get the desired information. With that it provides its users with different causes, where you educate others, other than your friends, about your point of view on certain issue. Rather, you can create your own world on Facebook, where all happens according to your wish. Making Facebook your home, lets you live your viral life in a better way.

The Different Facebook Applications and Features

There are many different types of applications that are available on Facebook in order to help users be able to get in touch with one another. Most of these applications are available to all users, as well as some users have even made their own applications. In recognition of the ordinary users being able to make their own application on Facebook, there was an announcement made at the annual conference on July 23rd of 2008 regarding a new application called Facebook Connect. Facebook Connect is one of the newest applications which has been created and is available to everyone in December of 2008. What the service requires is for people to be able to sign on, browse other websites as well as other affiliated sites while using their Facebook account.

By being able to use their Facebook account, they can easily share new information from other websites directly onto their Facebook page as well as with their friends. Facebook Connect has started implementing its software with other websites and is soon going to be working at a full scale.

We will be covering most of the popular applications which have been created in order help Facebook; some have even become a very important factor which sets Facebook different from other social networking websites.

News Feed

The news feed was created by a man named Ruchi Sanghvi, on September 6th of 2006. The news feed is displayed on the user's home page right when Facebook users log directly into their account. This application easily provides new information as well as an updated list of all the activities that their friends' have been doing on Facebook while they were missing. It is basically used as an option to catch up to what the user might have missed out on. News Feed has certain information which it specifically makes sure to include within its updating continuously.

Certain specifics are the changes that their friends may make on their profile, birthday reminders popping up about their friends, upcoming events which they may be interested in, posts or comments on pictures, friends adding pictures on a Facebook album. One of the most interesting parts of Facebook is the fact that it can show the conversations which have been taking place between the user and his friends, as well as some mutual friends. A separate part of the News Feed is the Mini-Feed. The Mini-Feed is more a news stream which is on the user's profile page so that visitors or friends looking at the users profile page may be able to see what they have been doing on Facebook recently.

The Mini-Feed has one characteristic of feature which makes it different from the News Feed; that is the user has the ability or option to remove and delete events that are posted from the Mini-Feed even after they have done an action and it has appeared on the Mini-Feed. The reason behind this is that the Mini-Feed is able hide actions and makes them no longer visible to the visitors or friends that might view the profile later on.

With addition of the News Facebook, it was faced with some heavy criticism and discontent amongst the various different Facebook users. The usual complaints were that the News Feed was becoming too cluttered and sometimes had information posted which they were not interested in at all. Others were more concerned about the lack of privacy or invasion of privacy that the News Feed caused since it was now easy to track the activities of other friends. Activities which were even sometimes personal, such as the relationship status, different events they might be attending, as well as the whole conversation they might have had with another user on their wall.

Mark Zuckerberg, the creator Facebook, took a step forward and responded to these complaints with an apology and then later started to include options which where customizable to the user's privacy preference.

With this new addition and tool, the users were able to control which information and activities were automatically shared amongst friends. This was a major change in the entire way the software worked, and it was received and welcomed by Facebook users with a lot of enthusiasm. As of right now, the most recent Facebook is able to let users pick which friends are able to see what specific updates and activities that have been occurring about them. There have been several different options available as to how the user may want to control their own private activities, even though some of the major events cannot be controlled and managed by the user. Overall, this new capability within the News Feed was a major factor in separating its entire quality with other social networking websites.

The new ability and this new software produced an entire new look and redesigned all of the pages of Facebook. This is now considered the "New Facebook". There are many different new features which have changed with the News Feed. Some of the more common and loved ones by Facebook users was the fact that the users were given the option of removing any type of update from any other application that they might have had occurring. Along with that, the user was able to control the size of these news bulletins when they showed up on their page.

The most recent addition to this application was the fact that the users were able to choose what information that they are more interested in according to the specific friend. They can hear more or less from a friends fall depending on their relationship in real life.

Wall

The Facebook Wall is one of the oldest applications that have been used by Facebook users. This application uses up some of the space; almost most of the space, of the user's profile page and allows for others to post messages and comments for the user. The user is able to see what the message is, as well as the time and date of when it was written. The user can make this wall open for friends depending on the user's preference. The user's preference also allows keeping this application hidden from other friends or visitors. The Facebook Wall is mostly used amongst the general population of Facebook users in order to send general messages to and from one another. Depending on the preference of the person posting, they may either send a message privately which goes directly into the person's Inbox and can only be seen by that person.

It is a type of email or private communication for that person. As of 2007, in July the developers of Facebook started to allow users to be able to post attachments directly onto a person's wall. Before this, the wall was used and limited to only text content. The older the messages get, they are still saved, but pushed back onto an "archive" page which can easily be viewed again.

Photos

The one thing which is similar to other social networking websites, but is still considered to be one of a kind as well as one of the most popular applications is the Photo's Application of Facebook. It is a unique application which other social networking websites are lacking. With this application, users are able to upload albums of photo's directly onto Facebook, and then here is the unique factor, they are able to tag other friends directly on those pictures. Once they tag those friends on a photo, the friends are sent a notification and that picture gets added to that friend's photo album as well. The Facebook Photo application is all interlinked with one another. Users are able to tag friends, and then comment on the photos directly. These comments can lead to a wide range of discussions which can be entertaining and quite long lasting.

Just the statistics of this application are outstanding and overwhelming. These statistics compared to other social networking websites, are astonishing. Overall, there are nearly 1.7 billion user photos available on Facebook. Out of all of these photos, there are nearly 2.2 billion friends that have been tagged onto these photos. The whole amount of space which is being used by these photographs is nearly 160 terabytes of storage, where there's an additional 60 terabytes just waiting to be used. On a weekly basis, there are nearly more than 60 million photos added. Each week, nearly 5 terabytes of space is used up. On a daily basis, more than 3 billion photos are shared amongst users and viewed. More than 100,000 images are served every second during the peak time for Facebook. These statistics speak for themselves.

Gifts

Another very common application which was added onto Facebook in February of 2007 was the new gift feature. The gift feature allowed users and friends to purchase gifts, which have been small icons or pictures of special novelty items to one another. The design of these items and this application was created by none other than the former Apple designer Susan Kare. There is a virtual gift shop open and the user can easily send one another gifts as well as add a personalized message.

The gift then later on appears on the recipient's profile page with the message that the sender had sent. Another additional option when sending a message is to send a gift privately, in which case the name of the sender is not shown as well as the message being hidden from other uses. Overall, all the gifts start showing up on the person's profile page under a gift box. Each gift is marked below with the sender or a "private" label. The third option when sending a gift is to send it anonymously, in this option, anyone with profile access is able to see the gift entirely, but the message is set for private view just for the user. With the anonymous option, the receiver is also not able to see the sender's name. No one is able to see the name; however, the user can see the gift sitting in their gift box.

When a Facebook user activates their account they are able to send one free gift. Each additional gift costs nearly $1.00. The entire application was started around Valentines Day. All the revenue was taken, after the processing fees for credit cards were taken out, during the month of February 2007, and half of it was donated to the charity 'Susan G. Komen for the Cure'. After the month ended, there was no longer the charity donation. Right after that, Facebook started to make their gifts on a daily basis, with one new gift each day.

The way they were able to sell the gifts faster was to limit the supply as well as limit the availability for the time. Users purchased them rapidly in order to send them before other people end up using all the available supplies.

Recently this program took a change in the way it allowed users to purchase these gifts. Instead of purchasing the gifts for a dollar, they changed the type of payment model. On November 8th 2008, they changed it to a point system where the people paid a dollar for 100 points and used those points to send gifts. The application has plans to make a larger and more variety of gifts in the future.

There has been another application which has been created recently by another user, Zachary Allia. Zachary Allia had the idea of avoiding the payment for gifts. The only difference is that it is not the regular or official gifts that are sent through Facebook, and they are also displayed on Facebook in a completely different way.

Marketplace

Another great feature that Facebook added recently in 2007 was the Facebook Marketplace. Facebook Marketplace is a way for user's to post free classified ads for products. They can place ads in many different categories which include For Sale, Jobs, Housing, and many others. Ads can either be for things which are readily available or for users who are requiring something specifically. This feature, the marketplace, is readily available for use by any Facebook users and is entirely free of any cost.

Pokes

One distinctive feature of Facebook is the ability to poke people. Not literally though. The feature allows for one user to send another user on Facebook a "poke" which shows them they are either interested in talking to them or to just interact with your friends non-verbally. The Facebook staff created this process in order to have a distinctive feature without any specific purpose. They have purposed that people should have their own interpretation of poking between their friends. Having your own meaning amongst strangers or friends is a great way of creating an interesting and fun conversation. It is intended to be a nudge to let others know that you are interested or to get the attention of other users.

The term of poke has been used in the English language for many years with different meanings, some members on Facebook use it as a sexual advancement since it has a sexual meaning as well. Now on Facebook, there are several other applications which are readily available that have been created by other Facebook users. This allows users to put any type of action or verb in place of the poke and it creates a different type of unique fun amongst friends and strangers.

Status

The one great application which was added on for users to avail was the status update. Facebook created this feature in order for the user to be able to micro blog where the users are able to inform their friends about certain actions or thoughts. There can be a random different type of results depending on the user. These can be simple statements such as "Bob is sad" or "Bob is thinking about apple pie right now". The original status update was created with the persons user name following a 'is' to be filled out. Recently in December 2007, users had the ability to be able to remove the 'is' and put any other verb that they want to in creating a sentence. By default, the 'is' still appears but can easily be taken down. The recently updated section is consistently changed amongst friend's news feed and they are able to see.

Events

Facebook events were another application which was created for members of Facebook to be able to organize and advertise certain events which may be coming shortly within their society and community. It is a great way of organizing social gatherings which can include small house parties, club nights, birthday parties, or even something small like a gaming night amongst a bunch of guys. There are certain requirements as to the event application, such as having an event name, tagline, network, the host's name, the type of event it may be, the location and the city that the event may take place in, the start and end times of the event, as well as an invite to friends which later becomes a guest list. This application allows friends to either accept, decline, or reply with a maybe. Some of these applications can either be open for the ordinary public, be closed and need an invitation only, or be secret, like a surprise birthday party. When events are being set up, the users are allowed to upload videos, photos, as well as be able to post different items regarding the event.

Networks and Groups

The interesting part of Facebook is the ability that users are able to join different networks and groups accordingly to their preference and location.

There are many different privacy settings that can take place on these networks. Some groups are allowed to hold discussions as well as may inform group members about affiliating events that may be taking place locally. This is a great way for the people of the society to come together on a virtual land and share information with one another, as well as discuss some specific subjects. These networks and groups vary according to the location of the person to something as small as being a member of any type of club. Mostly companies and public relations use these types of services to attract members of different customers and consumers, as well as the ordinary public, employees of a firm, and members of any type of organization. The group is usually full of, and not limited to, members who have joined recently on their own, as well as the recent news regarding the group. There is also different types of discussion boards that are going along continuously amongst the members as well as a full out type of forum room. There are wall contents like you would see on a profile page, as well as pictures, recently posted items and videos.

Video

Right around the time that Facebook launched its original platform it included an application which wasn't as common. Recently the idea of sharing videos was increased thanks to websites mainly like Youtube.com.

Facebook has had that feature and ability to share videos amongst friends since it started. Users are able to add different types of videos with the help of this service. This service can easily upload videos from anywhere, as well as add video's directly from a mobile using Facebook Mobile. Another creative way of recording video and adding it directly onto Facebook is to use a person's webcam. Users are able to tag other friends like they are able to with the photo application. Just like the photo application, the users also get that video added onto their profile so that other friends may also take a look into what it is. Users have had the ability to send one another messages through video for a very long time thanks to this application.

Chat

One of the most recent changes to occur within Facebook occurred on April 5th of 2008. Facebook released a "test" Facebook chat. It became official and was added to everyone's profile in April of 2008. The chat was then used by all of the users. This gave users the ability to talk to one another on a one to one basis instead of writing on one another's wall waiting for a reply.

Instant messaging on Facebook made it even more unique compared to all the other social networking websites. The newest addition which the developers of this application are trying to do is to incorporate Facebook chat with other software's.

Advertising Solutions on Facebook

Advertising on social networks is not the same as advertising on a common search engine. Most companies get the impression that by getting more fans on Facebook, the better and more successful their social advertisement has become. Now advertising by using a banner and posting it on a site is becoming more outdated, thanks to Facebook. When online users click on an advertisement, they usually click on it for two reasons. They are either aware that it is an ad and it is relevant to them or they don't know that it is an ad but it is relevant to them. Now Facebook has created a system where companies and agencies can generate fans on a social network. When one user becomes a fan, the friends of that particular individual are notified right away. This is a form of a unique advertisement that is only available on face book. Through this news feed companies gin more popularity as more people become notified of their existence.

Facebook has become very easy to use over the past few years. Now, if you want to advertise on Facebook you first have to make an account for yourself and/or your company. When that is complete you go to advertise by clicking on of the buttons that say advertise. This will open a page that will show you a tutorial and walkthrough of how to set up your fan club.

FACEBOOK ADVANCED 2.0

There are a total of three buttons on the top of the page that are in this order, About Advertisement, Prepare, and Step by Step. The purpose of this is to help you gather all the information you need in order to create an ad on Facebook. When you click on About Advertisement, it gives you all the points that you should keep in mind when creating your ad and why you should keep track of it. Here are some examples of what to keep in mind when creating an ad on face book.

- Create an image based ad
- Target the users precisely by their age, gender, location, etc.
- Attach some social actions related to your business
- Generate more demand for your product and services with relevant ads
- Track your progress with real reporting
- Get insight on who is clicking and shy
- Customize your ads to get the best results

The next tab is Prepare. This takes you to a page that talks about the links, images, and messages that you will post on your ad. At the bottom left, there will be a blue button that reads Get Started. This will take you to the same page as the Create an Ad button does.

The Step by Step tab shows the steps needed to be taken in order to create an ad that will run continuously on Facebook.

Here are the steps from Step by Step, respectively. First, you have to decide if you want the users to be directed to your own web page or to an application on Facebook. The next step would be to create an ad. There are a few guidelines for this. Certain aspects of your ads should be consistent so that they could attract the targeted audience. For example, the title of your ad needs to be at least 25 characters in length, including spaces. The body of the ad should be at the most, 135 characters in length, including spaces. There should also be an image or photo to go with your ad. There is a special system on Facebook where you can add special actions on the ads you create. The friends of the audiences will be notified if there are any interactions with the client and the company/brand. The third step in creating your ad on Facebook involves the targeting of a specific age group, sex, location, work place, relationship status, relationship interest, education level, etc. Be sure to target your audience with demographic and psychographic filters about real life services/people. The targeting page is set to default for people that are 18 years of age or older. This usually applies to the US and Canada only.

However, you should modify your ads in order to reach all the people within the specific age groups. Be sure to make an estimate of how many people will match your criteria. The fourth and most important step, you now have to decide whether to pay for your ad per clicks or per views. Be sure to choose an appropriate payment tab. If you want more information on prices and payments, check the Facebook FAQ. After you decide how you want to pay for your advertisement, you need to decide on how much you want to spend on your ad per day. You will also have to estimate the maximum payment for a thousand impressions. You will also be informed of how much other advertisers are bidding for their ads as well. Now set a schedule for your ad and we're done here.

Now the last step is to check your ads for errors. If there is information that you need to change, just click on change ad and fix your. Now your ad is ready ad to be shown on Facebook.

Personalization

Social networking websites were made part of the internet a very long time ago. However, with the passage of time they have been improving as with the improvement in technology. Most of all, every new website came with a new level of personalization. Personalization, where your homepage literally becomes your home and everything happens just like as you would prefer in your home.

Facebook came up with the highest level of personalization making it possible to treat your homepage as your home. When the users registered with Facebook, they were free to choose application that matches their interest. Facebook provides different options to the users among which they can choose easily. If the user thinks that he can create something for himself and others as well, he is free to do so. Facebook provides him the possible support in the creation of application and communicating the application to other Facebook users as well.

However Facebook platform has been working to provide the most personalized services to the Facebook users. Facebook is available in 35 different translations. 60 more are in the development process. These translations are the part of personalization, as these translations provide users from different cultures with the facility to use Facebook in their own language. Programmers and developers from all over the world are working on the Facebook platform on a daily basis. This diverse workforce of Facebook facilitates the users to personalize their accounts on special cultural and geographical events as well.

Religious groups and applications created by users from different religions are being used by the people to show their affiliation and respect for them. Other personalized applications, like bumper stickers, are also provided to the Facebook users. Bumper stickers talks about the personality of the users with some message or images used in it. Users can also create their own bumper sticker. Other than that, users can easily choose to update their profile by adding new games, groups, photos, and status changes.

Fight Over Facebook

On a long sunny afternoon near downtown Palo Alto, California, the collaborators of Facebook are arranging their headquarters for a huge party to celebrate Facebook's four year anniversary. There were lights being strung up by workmen and tables were being arranged with champagne glasses.

Even then, the CEO was nowhere to be found. He was sitting in a small cubicle in an office located in a building that was a little far off from Sanford University. He was oblivious to the preparations that were being made. He sits in his glass walled office, eating his take out order. He looks more like a little kid who is just pondering about random topics. He doesn't give us the impression that he is the founder of a social networking website that is worth just as much as the General motors company

Zuckerberg has made millions off of his idea, Facebook. He is called the Bill Gates of his generation. The Harvard dropout is also facing many allegations of stealing the ideas from others. During the case, one of the judges described it as a blood feud.

Three of his fellow peers from Harvard claim that Zuckerberg fleeced the idea from them after he created a code for a social networking site that they were working on. Also, in April, another classmate filed a petition to cancel Facebook's trademark. Aaron Greenspan claimed that he had created an online Facebook months before Zuckerberg had.

These legal challenges that Zuckerberg has to face painted a curious image of a man who has now become in charge of our social future. The world's most popular networking tool was created by a brilliant nerd who did nothing but sit all alone in his dorm room. He is described as the super dork of this digital age. No matter what the outcome of the legal dispute turns out to be, it raises one huge question. Was the Facebook Empire founded on a crime?

Facebook was born under many disputed circumstances. During the fall of 2003, the scope of online social networking just started to grow. Mark Zuckerberg has always had a competitive streak that combined with his love for technology.

However, when he entered Harvard, he was surrounded with hundreds of other freshmen who had resumes as good and through as his. When he needed an identity within the campus, he mad a site called Facesmash. This ended because the school made it stop and let Mark go with just a warning.

Currently, the owners of a rival social networking website are trying to shut down Facebook. They are claiming that the idea was stolen from them. Now a federal judge delayed the ruling of whether accepting the lawsuit filed against Mark Zuckerberg. It is said that there is not enough information on the allegations and that they cannot prove if Mark Zuckerberg is guilty or not.

Future of Facebook

Facebook has integrated itself into everyday life just as completely as computers and the Internet has. The convenience and ease it offers in providing social connectivity has made it an instant hit and it continues to grow from its present base of 30 million users. Facebook has grown from its humble beginnings as a Harvard-only interface for students to keep in touch with each other, to one which offers global connectivity and allows friends to stay in touch with each other even if they are continents apart. The breakneck rate of growth has left its competitors like MySpace far behind, with the amount of users doubling every six months.

This exponential growth has been primarily due to a lack of alternatives for people to achieve what it provides. Facebook does not try and build a social community from scratch. It only serves to help people get in touch with each other.

The fact that it builds on already existing relationships means that people do not have any incentive to act or portray themselves as anything else. This allows an authenticity which is absent from most other social networking websites and thus does not make people wary of using it. It also increases their disposition towards helping create a friendly and hospitable environment so that they and their friends remain comfortable while using Facebook.

The company's CEO, Mark Zuckerberg, has continued to rebuff offers from potential buyers, since his vision is to make the company a part of everyone's lives and to let it continue to provide utility as effectively as it does today. The value of this utility can be gauged by the amount of the offers, with Viacom putting $750 million and Yahoo $1 billion. Zuckerberg has stated that he is in no hurry to sell off the company and considering that the venture started off only 2 years ago, it does make sense for him to continue to build it. Furthermore, his investors who have put up $38 million into the venture remain confident about its growth potential.

An indication of how much potential the company has is the interest shown by the launch of Facebook Platform. This has allowed non Facebook developers, to build applications and utilities which are reliant on Facebook.

The result has seen interested companies building whole new products which cater to Facebook and which provide services based on Facebook. In fact, there has already been a phone launched with it focus on Facebook connectivity. This has not only helped Facebook's popularity but also provided users with different ways to use it. The growth in popularity has also seen it grow internationally. It already has 10% to 15 % of the population in Canada and it is building on its substantial base in the UK as well.

However, for it to remain growing at the same rate, Facebook will need to keep providing its users the ease of use and comfort that it has. Managing that with the amount of users already on Facebook and the commercial and advertising interests will prove difficult but Zuckerberg and his investors remain confident. At present, the future of Facebook looks extremely bright.

THE END

FACEBOOK ADVANCED 2.0

The following few pages are used for Book & Search Engines only. The top Google Search terms for "Facebook" are below

6 degrees of separation, 6 degrees of separation book, about face book, aboutface, adult face book, advertising, an awesome, and mark zuckerberg, application, are you looking for, austin peay, bebo.com, biosilk, block face book, blog, blogger, blogging, blogs, booj, bookk, bookl, boook, borekas, bppl, business networking, buy books, came here, canopy club, cars, cat book face book, cat face book, chasing the wind, chat, chat room, chhibber, chris hughes, classmates, college, college face book, collegefacebook, com, community, connectu, create a face book, create face book, creating a face book, customize face book, date, dating, dating sites, download, dunster house, dupre face book, ebay, eisenhower auditorium, email, events, fac ebook, facbook, face audiobook, face authentication, face booj, face book, face book a, face book accounts, face book add ons, face book ads, face book at work, face book bad, face book badge, face book blog, face book book, face book ca, face book canada, face book co, face book co uk, face book codes, face book com, face book com log in, face book come, face book comm, face book con, face book contact, face book directory, face book en espanol, face book espanol, face book expressions, face book fan, face book flair, face book fly, face book for dummies, face book for kids, face book france, face book friends, face book groups, face book high school, face book highschool, face book home, face book hot, face book how to, face book im, face book images, face book ip adress, face book job, face book layouts, face book link, face book list, face book log in, face book login, face book mail, face book me, face book mobile, face book ocm, face book om, face book or, face book org, face book owner, face book pages, face book people, face book phone, face book photo, face book picture, face book poking, face book privacy, face book profiles, face book proxy, face book register, face book sale, face book search, face book sign in, face book sign up, face book social networking, face book sold, face book statuses, face book stickers, face book stuff, face book things, face book uk, face book value, face book video, face book wall, face bookk, face bookl, face boook, face bppl, face college, face friends, face harvard, face high school, face highschool, face login, face me, face ook, face people, face social networking, facebook, facebooks, facebooks com, faces hardcover, familiar faces, find face book, find friends, flickr, flippin, free, free dating, free face book, friend, friends, fun, g face book, games, get a face book, get to face book, girls, gmail, google, google face book, grimlins, harvard crimson, harvard face book, harvard university, hephaiston, hi5, hi5.com, high school, highschool, hotmail, how mark zuckerberg, http, i didn t, i m, i remember, internet, internet dating, jet man face book, jill foster, job, join face book, kids face

book, know each other, kootali face book, leverett, lidsky, linked in, lions and tigers, little face book, login, lore lay, love, m face book, make a face book, make face book, make friends, make money, make money online, marc zuckerberg, mark zuckerberg, mark zuckerberg contact, mark zuckerberg email, mark zuckerberg girlfriend, mark zuckerberg interview, mark zuckerberg net, mark zuckerberg net worth, mark zuckerberg of, mark zuckerberg speaks, mark zuckerberg wiki, mark zuckerberg wikipedia, mark zuckerberg worth, marketing, mcginity, me, meet friends, meet people, mi face book, microsoft, mixtapeone, mobile, money, more friends, movies, mp3, msn, mt holyoke, music, music for face book, music on face book, my face book, my face book com, my face book page, myfacebook, myspace posters, myspaces, myspaces com, myucdavis, nerfu, network, networking, networking site, news, no face book, no face book com, north face book bags, nunc scio quit sit amor, obama, ogin, old face book, online community, online dating, online social networking, orkut, owned face book, pacific lutheran, people, people book, personals, pet face book, pictures, pictures for face book, pictures on face book, poking, police face book, popped collar, profile, profiles, proxy, rensselaer polytech, saverin, school, sign up for face book, silk therapy, similar to face book, singles, smcm, smcm face book, social, social media, social network, social networking, social networking site, social networks, social utility, sports, sposit, stalkernet, stuff for face book, suny potsdam, tagworld, the best site ever, the face book, the face book com, the world face book, theface, theface book, thefacebok, thefacebook, thefacebook book, things for face book, tulier, twitter, two face book, uillinois, un block face book, unblock, unblock face book, unblocked face book, uoguelph, used books, utube, uvac, video, video on face book, videos, viewstar, vintage face book, web 2.0, web design, west morris central, what is face book, who created face book, who owns face book, wii, winklevoss, wirehog, women, work from home, world face book, ww face book, ww face book com, www, www face book, www face book co, www face book com, www facebooks, www facebooks com, www my face book, www thefacebook, wwww face book, wwww face book com, yalestation, yellow book, you face book, you tube, you tube face book, young audiences, youtube, youtube.com, yuwie, zi wei, zuckerberg, zuckerberg face book

The common mis-spellings of "Facebook", "Face Book", and "Facebook.com"

facebook, acebook, fcebook, faebook, facbook, faceook, facebok, faceboo, afcebook, fcaebook, faecbook, facbeook, faceobook, faceboko, ffacebook, faacebook, faccebook, faceebook, facebbook, facebooook, facebookk, dacebook, gacebook, fscebook, faxebook, favebook, facwbook, facrbook, facevook, facenook, facebiok, facebpok, facebook, facebopk, facebooj,

FACEBOOK ADVANCED 2.0

facebool, racebook, tacebook, vacebook, cacebook, fqcebook, fwcebook, fzcebook, fadebook, fafebook, fac3book, fac4book, facdbook, facsbook, facegook, facehook, faceb9ok, faceb0ok, faceblok, facebkok, facebo9k, facebo0k, facebolk, facebokk, facebooi, facebooo, faceboom, face book, book face, ace book, fce book, fae book, fac book, face ook, face bok, face boo, afce book, fcae book, faec book, face obok, face boko, fface book, faace book, facce book, facee book, face bbook, face boook, face bookk, dace book, gace book, fsce book, faxe book, fave book, facw book, facr book, face vook, face nook, face biok, face bpok, face boik, face bopk, face booj, face bool, race book, tace book, vace book, cace book, fqce book, fwce book, fzce book, fade book, fafe book, fac3 book, fac4 book, facd book, facs book, face gook, face hook, face b9ok, face b0ok, face blok, face bkok, face bo9k, face bo0k, face bolk, face bokk, face booi, face booo, face boom, facebookcom, acebookcom, fcebookcom, faebookcom, facbookcom, faceookcom, facebokcom, faceboocom, facebookom, facebookcm, facebookco, afcebookcom, fcaebookcom, faecbookcom, facbeookcom, faceobokcom, facebokocom, faceboockom, facebookocm, facebookcmo, ffacebookcom, faacebookcom, faccebookcom, faceebookcom, facebbookcom, faceboookcom, facebookkcom, facebookccom, facebookcoom, facebookcomm, dacebookcom, gacebookcom, fscebookcom, faxebookcom, favebookcom, facwbookcom, facrbookcom, facevookcom, facenookcom, facebiokcom, facebpokcom, faceboikcom, facebopkcom, faceboojcom, faceboolcom, facebookxom, facebookvom, facebookcim, facebookcpm, facebookcon, racebookcom, tacebookcom, vacebookcom, cacebookcom, fqcebookcom, fwcebookcom, fzcebookcom, fadebookcom, fafebookcom, fac3bookcom, fac4bookcom, facdbookcom, facsbookcom, facegookcom, facehookcom, faceb9okcom, faceb0okcom, faceblokcom, facebkokcom, facebo9kcom, facebo0kcom, facebolkcom, facebokkcom, facebooicom, faceboooom, faceboomcom, facebookdom, facebookfom, facebookc9m, facebookc0m, facebookclm, facebookckm, facebookcoj, facebookcok

FACEBOOK ADVANCED 2.0

Books > Computers & Internet > Software > Business > Utilities

Books > Computers & Internet > Networking > Networks, Protocols & APIs

Books > Computers & Internet > Business & Culture > Web Marketing

- Internet
- World Wide Web (WWW)
- Computer network resources
- Design
- Online social networks
- Social networks
- Web sites
- Social Institutions
- Computers
- Computer - Internet
- Computer Books: Web Publishing
- Computers / Interactive & Multimedia
- Computers / Internet / General
- Computers / Internet / World Wide Web
- Computers / Social Aspects / General
- Computers / Utilities
- Interactive & Multimedia
- Internet - World Wide Web
- Social Aspects - General
- Web - General
- Computing: Consumer Books ('Technical Trade')